DIVINE
CONNECTION

WHEN THE SUPERNATURAL
BECOMES ... NATURAL

María de Jesús Alarcón L.

WESTBOW
PRESS®
A DIVISION OF THOMAS NELSON
& ZONDERVAN

WestBow Press books may be ordered through booksellers or by contacting:

WestBow Press
A Division of Thomas Nelson & Zondervan
1663 Liberty Drive
Bloomington, IN 47403
www.westbowpress.com
1 (866) 928-1240

Scripture taken from the King James Version of the Bible.

Scripture taken from the New King James Version®. Copyright © 1982 by Thomas Nelson. Used by permission. All rights reserved.

ISBN: 978-1-9736-8059-8 (sc)
ISBN: 978-1-9736-8060-4 (e)

Library of Congress Control Number: 2019919449

Print information available on the last page.

WestBow Press rev. date: 1/20/2020

I DEDICATE THIS BOOK WITH GRATITUDE

TO MY HEAVENLY FATHER
THE ONE WHO LOVES ME THE MOST

TO JESUS MY SAVIOR
THE ONE WHO DIED FOR MY SINS
ON THE CROSS

TO THE HOLY SPIRIT
MY FAITHFUL COMPANION

ALL THINGS ARE POSSIBLE
WHEN WE HAVE DIVINE CONNECTION!

Dear Friend,

I pray that the message in this book will impact your life and your future the way that has impacted my own life.

My personal journey has been written with the intention to share a new found awareness, after my Divine Connection.

Now, I am able to recognize that many of my experiences have been uncommon.

Till now, I have been spared from dying seven times, and in one of those occasions I was taken to Heaven and given the option to stay in heaven, or come back to Earth.

After my visit to Heaven, I discovered a new path that I didn't know existed. I suddenly became aware that I had a personal mission to fulfill here on the Earth, and what I needed to do, was to follow the path that would take me into my personal assignment.

DURING MY CHILDHOOD

I THOUGHT THAT I WAS LIVING

IN THE WRONG WORLD

I DIDN'T FIT IN

UNTIL I DISCOVER THE REASON

I DISCOVERED…

THAT WE HAVE ENTERED THE WORLD

HOLDING A PESONAL GIFT FROM HEAVEN

GIVEN BY OUR HEAVENLY FATHER

THE GIFT IS TO BE SHARED
WITH THE WORLD

EVEN IF THE WRAPPING
AND COLOR OF THE GIFT IS DIFFERENT

ALL OF THE GIFTS ARE UNIQUE!

And God saw everything that he had made,
and behold it was very good. Genesis 1:31

MY PERSONAL GIFT TO
SHARE WITH THE WORLD

My arrival into the world was a surprise to my parents;
they were expecting a Son,
And here I was, another daughter arriving to fulfill my
personal Mission on the Earth.
During my childhood, the first thing that I noticed was
the feeling of an empty space
Inside me, as if something was missing.

During this time, I didn't have a sense of direction
regarding my life and my future. No
Plans, No Dreams, or Desires. No matter where I was,
I didn't fit in.
My existence in the world was a mystery to me. I was
only following a daily routine.
It took over thirty years to find the reason for feeling
different from other people.

My discovery happened, when I became aware that right after we enter the world,
Our personal Gift from Heaven becomes activated; to guide us and prepare us.

While seeking for my personal Mission, I discovered that all of us arrived into the
World with an empty space inside our hearts... and over the years, I noticed the
Different ways that we use, trying to fill the empty space:

One of them is by eating Meals or snacks without being hungry, hopping to fill the space.

Another way is by listening to Music. We listen to songs that remind us of a pleasant
Experience with a person that we love, and play the Songs over and over, trying to
Fill the empty feeling with pleasant memories.

The person who experiences the empty space with sadness, their way to forget is by
Drinking Alcohol, using Drugs, or seeking intimate relations for distraction. They are desperately trying to silence the voice that keeps reminding them about

the empty space. Some addictions can be the reason for trying to fill the empty space.

When I think about the past, I remember that most of my life I have been doing unexpected things; one of those things, was moving from one Country (Mexico), to live in another Country that spoke a different language (USA). Always surprising my family with something different from what they expected. It looked as if I never acted "normal" unaware that I was searching for my mission on the Earth.

My move to the USA was planned perfectly like a Puzzle, with everything that needed to happen. My Heavenly Father gather together all of the pieces for the unforeseen event. This was part of my assignment.

All began at the age of twelve, when Hurricane Hilda arrived to Tampico Mexico, the place where I lived with my parents. The Hurricane entered our town swiftly with strong wind and heavy rain, flooding most of the streets.

After many days of rain and flooded roads, our food supply was getting low; we, the children, could see our parents concerned about not having enough food for us, and shortly after, we encounter an unexpected surprise...

It was early afternoon when we heard the sound of helicopters. We ran outdoors to see what they were doing, and watched how three Helicopters from the United States of America, were dropping boxes filled with food for all of us. This was one unforgettable experience for me! This event brings tears to my eyes every time

I think about the experience…

While watching the Helicopters dropping the boxes with food, a dream was born inside my heart, **a desire that seemed like an impossible dream;** to be able to live among people that care about the well- being of others. This was the way that I was raised by my Parents.

Four years later, my friend Rachel approaches me asking if I would be interested to have a friend from the USA. I quickly said yes, and she gave me his name and address. We began to get to know each other by mail; he was writhing to me in Spanish.

While writing, Peter shared that he was serving in the USA Military, flying helicopters, and continued to say, that being a pilot was a dream come true for him, that he wanted to fly airplanes since a young boy, born in Europe. He said that some of his friends would laugh at his words... while sharing about his dream, but his desire was much greater than their words... After writhing to each other for twelve months, he decided to visit Mexico for us to meet in person, and three days after his arrival he wanted to get married.

Now, the impossible dream was a reality, and the supernatural was natural.
My heavenly Father granted the desires of my heart, and the following day after our marriage, I arrived to the USA at the age of 18.

Delight yourself also in the lord, and He shall give you the desires of your heart.
God's Word was manifesting in my life! Psalm 37: 4 NKJV

I am still amazed, about how our Heavenly Father found the way to unite us in Matrimony, even when we lived in faraway countries from each other. I am thankful that He wanted for our children to be born in this wonderful Country, the United States of America!

I would like to express my gratitude, to all of you, the people that have built this Country for what it is today, a Christian Nation that loves our Creator, and always willing to help people in need… I am forever thankful to be living among all of you! God Bless you!

Dear friend, I didn't know that the life that I am now living existed. What a big surprise! I discover the person that loves us the most, and that person is by our side daily… I encountered His Presence and His Love!

MY FIRST ENCOUNTER WITH HIS PRESENCE

It happened one morning after my husband left for work. That day, while doing the daily chores, I remembered sitting on the living room sofa, folding the clean laundry, when suddenly, all I could see was darkness. I lost my eyesight instantly.

The experience of not being able to see the light impacted me greatly. Fear and Panic almost took over me. I quickly stood up from the sofa and began to walk towards the front door to call for help. While walking towards the door, I was holding tightly to the furniture that was in my path to avoid falling.

When I finally reached the front door, I grabbed the doorknob and opened the door, and at that instant, I recovered my eyesight. I closed the door and sat on the sofa and began to weep, after becoming aware that if I had taken one step outside the door, I would have fallen down the steps.

In a moment of panic, I had forgotten that we lived on the second floor. This happened while expecting our first child. I was six months pregnant.

That day, Jesus was revealing to me that I was not alone; just because I count see him with my eyesight! Now, I was able to recognize that Jesus was the one who protected me from falling down the steps. He always arrives on time!

God's Word, was manifesting once again... **Jesus said to him,** "Thomas," because you have seen me, you have believed. Blessed are those who have not seen, and yet have believed. John 20:29 NKJV

MY SECOND ENCOUNTER WITH JESUS CHANGED MY LIFE!

That day, I was praying and crying after the loss of family members including my little girl Nancy, twenty two months of age, dying accidentally in one day.

I remember that I was pleading for Divine help with my whole heart; trying to reach beyond Planet Earth. **I needed to reach the place where the impossible becomes possible!** I needed help to ease the pain of my broken heart; I was discouraged thinking that my heart would never mend.

That day, while crying, I suddenly sensed a presence entering the room, saturating the atmosphere with a pleasant fragrance, as if I was sitting by a garden filled with many delicate white flowers! At that moment the room became silent and I began to pray with words coming from my heart. Without knowing, I was giving my life to Jesus… After praying, I heard His voice saying: "Now you are a Christian."

I was not aware of the significance about being a Christian. No one had spoken to me about it. It took a couple of months to discover the meaning, it happened while watching the 700 Club on television. It means to receive Jesus inside our heart, proclaiming that He is our Lord, our God, and Savior, and for us to begin a brand New Life. Leaving the past behind, and starting a new personal relationship with Him.

After praying, His love and Peace embraced me, and discovered that the empty space inside my heart was filled with His presence, and suddenly a Miracle happened! Jesus instantly dried my tears and mended my heart!

The following day, I was a happy person, smiling and speaking to everyone, the shyness that I had, left me. I was a brand new woman. I discovered that my experience was a Divine Resurrection. "Born Again Christian"
Now my Real self was being revealed. I had been released from my old self, to become the new original Maria, created in God's image…and began to live my life, from the inside of me… ready to learn how to be led by Jesus presence.

I always knew that Jesus loves all of us, but I thought that He was living in Heaven. Now I know that He's always by our side, ready to help us when we call on his name with our whole heart, reaching beyond Planet Earth, asking for what we need.

I want you to know that **JESUS** is real and wants to be our best friend. I remember the many times when I experienced the gentle touch of His hand on my hands while praying, He's always with us. Ask Him for what you need, and He will give it to you in his time, if it's for your good, and don't forget ... Jesus always arrives on time!

Jesus words: Ask, and it will be given to you; Seek and you will find; Knock and it will be opened to you. For everyone who asks receives. And he who seeks finds. And to him who knocks at the door will be opened. Matthew 7:7-8 NKJV

Jesus is saying: Ask for what you need, and it will be given to you; Seek me sincerely with your whole heart and you will find me; Knock at my heart door, and it will be opened to you. For everyone who asks receives; and he who seeks finds, and to him who knocks at my heart door, the door will be opened. Matt 7:7-8 NKJV

I was not aware that our lives can be changed in a matter of minutes in a surprising way. That day when it happened to me, everything seemed the same as the day before, and suddenly the help that I needed arrived in a matter of minutes.

I remember reaching out to Heaven with all of my heart, not knowing that I was connecting to the Heavenly Kingdom? Now I know that Jesus is our Divine Connection... when the Supernatural, becomes Natural... This awareness has been a Huge Blessing to me, like a Rainbow after the Rain.

My personal encounters with Jesus, motivates me to seek His presence with my whole heart. Now my greatest desire is to follow Him and get to know him as a friend.

Till now, Jesus has protected my life from dying seven times!

Dear friend, I don't know where you are, or what you need, but He knows. **Jesus** is always by your side, and His love for you is unconditional, you don't need to be perfect to approach Him. Just call on His name with your whole heart! He wants to help you, and he wants to be your best friend.

Jesus words: I am with you always even to the end of the world. Matth.28:20 NKJV

Over the years, I began to discover that our Creator (God) uses many different ways to help us discern our personal Gift from heaven, Our mission on the Earth.

God send an Angel to a young Godly woman, named Mary, to announce His plans regarding the birth of His only begotten Son Jesus. This was Mary's heavenly Gift.

Our Heavenly Father gave us His most valuable Gift ...**His only begotten Son, Jesus.** When Jesus entered the world as a baby, he was also holding a Gift from Heaven to share with the world. He Shared the Greatest Gift that we could have ever received: The gift of Salvation for a brand New Life.

For God so loved the world... that He gave His only begotten Son, that whoever believes in Him should not perish but have everlasting life. For God did not send His Son into the world to condemn the world. But that the world through Him might be saved. John 3:16 NKJV

Our Heavenly Father watched His own Son, carrying the Cross to Calvary. He could see the abuse on His Son's body, and heard the laughter of his abusers; He watched when the nails on his hands and feet were penetrating his body.

Our Heavenly Father endured watching the suffering of his only Son, to set us Free from Sin. He experienced all of these, because of His Love for Us.

All of us need Jesus to enter Heaven!

Jesus words: I AM THE WAY, THE TRUTH AND THE LIFE! No one comes to the Father except through Me. John 14:6. NKJV

In the Book of John, third chapter, **Jesus speaks about the New Birth (Divine Resurrection).** While speaking to Nicodemus, Jesus answered and said to him, most assuredly, I say to you, unless one is born again, he cannot see the kingdom of God. John 3:3 NKJV

Jesus said, that which is born of the flesh, is flesh, and that which is born of the spirit is spirit. Do not marvel that I said to you "you must be born again." This means receiving Jesus as our Lord and Savior for the forgiveness of our Sins, to be able to be born again in the Spirit… John 3:6-7 NKJV

The price that Jesus paid for our Salvation was Huge! When He was born, he entered the world like all of us, with a human body. He needed to be human like us, to pay for our human sins.

Jesus endured all of the pain on our behalf. He took our place to pay for our debt of Sin in full. Jesus is the only one, who can remove our Sins, and redeem our lives. When we receive Jesus in our hearts, and confess and believe that He is our Savior, at that moment we receive the cleansing of our Sins, to be able to enter Heaven.

When Jesus was living on the Earth like a human person, he encountered difficult times the same as us. It is for this reason, that He understands when we are in need of help. He's always willing to help us if we call on His name.

I remember when I discovered that all of us arrived into the World with the empty space inside our hearts, making us feel incomplete. In my daily life, I have encountered people feeling out of place, the way that I used to feel. Now I know that the solution is to pray the Miracle prayer with our whole Heart sincerely!

Often, after sharing the Miracle Prayer many people have asked: how did you know that I needed this prayer? My answer is always the same; Jesus knows what each one of us need. I have been sharing the Miracle Prayer everywhere I go for the past thirty years, and since then, I became aware that Jesus always arrives on time, to answer our need. Praise you Lord Jesus!

After saying the prayer, you will experience a Miracle, all of your Sins will be forgiven and removed, and the Peace of Jesus will be inside your heart. At that moment your brand New life begins, and Jesus will help you find your mission on the Earth.

Pray this prayer with **your whole heart**
and receive what you need!

Prayer for a brand new Life

Dear Lord Jesus,
I come before you, just as I am,
I repent of my sins, forgive me.
I invite you into my heart
And receive you as my Lord, God and Savior.
Cleanse me with your Divine blood,
And baptize me with your Holy Spirit.
I thank you Lord Jesus, for my Salvation. Amen.

After praying the Prayer, begin to read the Bible...

The Bible has been written by God, for all of us, expressing His Love, His Wisdom, and Guidance. He selected the right people to write it on his behalf.

Now, you can ask Jesus to help you find the right Bible for you. Visit a Christian book store, and when you find the Bible that is for you, embrace it and feel the peace of Jesus in it. Now you can start conversing with Jesus as your best friend, believing that He is listening to everything that you are saying. In time you will hear his voice coming from within yourself. He wants to help you find your mission on the Earth. Expect pleasant Surprises!

During the preparation for my Mission on the Earth; I became aware that I needed to capture every experience that I have lived during my life time. I needed to embrace every feeling, every emotion, every hurt and disappointment by the things that I saw, the words I heard, and the pain of a broken heart. I needed to remember all of this experiences to help people during difficult times; for me to be able to say "I know how you feel" This is one part of my Mission on the Earth. I needed to capture Jesus' likeness, to share His love, and compassion with the people who are experiencing difficult times.

While growing up, my Parents were good models for me. Since my childhood, I remember seeing my Mother feeding the people who knocked at the door, asking for something to eat. After eating my mother would shared with them about Jesus with encouraging words for a better future…

My mother was helping with the preparation for my Assignment. I was learning simply by observing what she was doing in my presence.

I also remember contemplating my father helping people in need. My father was a Carpenter; he built beautiful furniture made with Cedar wood that lasted for many generations. Some of my father's furniture was hand carved. He inherited this wonderful Gift from my Grandfather.

Many times, I observed my father providing work to people in need, and for the people unable to work because of an illness, He would give them money to go to the doctor or to buy medication. My Father's Gift to share with the world, was to treat God's Creation as family members.

And now, after waiting for instructions regarding my Assignment, the answer finally arrived, and appeared with a surprising revelation!

It was mid-morning when I was checking the mailbox. By this time I had already discovered the blessing of waking up to a brand new day...daily! I was amazed that our Heavenly Father makes every single day brand new! Now I know that we can live our daily lives with expectancy; by knowing that many wonderful changes can happen at any time.

After discovering this Truth, I was filled with Hope, by being aware that our lives can change in one single day! It can happen while experiencing difficult times. God's love for us endures forever!

I was learning that many of God's ways are unusual. Sometimes we are not sure about what He is saying to us, the importance of spending time alone with Him, seeking His guidance to help us understand His Plan for our lives.

God speaking: For my thoughts are not your thoughts, nor are your ways my ways, says the Lord. For as the heavens are higher than the earth, so are My ways higher than your ways, and my thoughts than your thoughts. Isaiah 55:8-9 NKJV

Some of the ways that God uses to communicate with us can be: by sending Angels with a message or sending his angels to protect us and to help us in our daily lives. He can also lead us by speaking directly to us, or speak to us while sleeping through visions and Dreams, or by using our eyesight.

I have personally experienced this different ways of communication with God, and still many more ways.

MY FIRST ENCOUNTER WITH ANGELS

That night I was asleep and also aware of their presence in my bedroom. One of the Angels approached me, and gave me a message. I still remember what he said to me. That night, the Angels filled my bedroom with bright light. I remember trying to get up, to turn the lights off, thinking that the lights in my room were on.

MY ENCOUNTER WITH GUARDIAN ANGELS

It happened while driving with my husband to the grocery store. This incident was presented to us suddenly unable to avoid.

That day, the road seemed empty, with the exception of one car driving at a distance on the opposite side of the road. While conversing with my husband, we both got distracted not paying attention to the road, until the car that was driving on the opposite side changed lanes, and it seemed as if the driver had lost control of the car, and now was driving on the same lane, facing us at high speed.

At that moment, my husband didn't have much time to do anything; the car was right in front of us; and at that instant I thought, "This is it, the last day of our lives" unaware that our Guardian Angels were present to protect us, by changing the outcome of this event; and suddenly everything changed swiftly with only few inches before touching our car. The car changed direction and landed outside the road.

JESUS ALWAYS ARRIVES ON TIME!

ANGELS TRAVELING WITH US

This experience happened when my husband and I, visit the country of Iran after being invited to their Industrial Exposition. Our company fabricated Hydraulic equipment designed by my husband.

I remember that as soon as we arrived to Iran, we were made aware of a bomb threat. We needed to wear a badge with our picture at all times.

The exposition was very interesting; I was amazed about how some people have the capability of creating a machine that would make a colorful material design, with many different colors to create woman's clothing.

The first three days, everything was fine, moving forward according to the way that we had planned, and suddenly, two days before our departure, we encountered the event that made us aware about God's Divine Protection. It was early afternoon, when we heard people yelling out loud and running towards one specific direction. A couple of hours later we were told that they apprehend the man that was putting the Bomb together, that he was caught on time.

After the exposition was over, we traveled to Israel... Many places in Israel, reminded me of the pictures that I have seen in the Bible. Was a pleasant experience

Now, it was time to return to The United States. As soon as we got home, my husband turned the television on to hear the latest news, and both of us got a big surprise, when we heard that in Israel at the Airport where we waited for our Plane hours earlier, a group of man entered with guns and killed many people.

God speaking to all of us: Because he hath set his love upon me, therefore I will deliver him: I will set him on high, because he knows my name. He shall call upon me, and I will answer him: I will be with him in trouble; I will deliver him, and honor him. Psalm 91:14-15 NKJV

THE ANGEL KNOCKING AT MY DOOR

It was early afternoon while getting ready to go out for a walk. My friend Cathy had already arrived and I was putting my shoes on, when suddenly the doorbell rang. I was surprised. I wasn't expecting anyone.

I opened the door and there he was, a nice looking young man smiling, saying that he was raising money to help the Russian people, and continued to say that for every donation he was giving a gift. He reached into the bag that he was holding and took different items out of the bag, mostly pictures of beautiful scenes.

I asked him to sit down and share what he had done to help others. He quickly responded that he needed to go, that other people were in the neighborhood helping and that they will be looking for him.

I gave him a donation, and while he was showing me the different items that I could have from the gift, I noticed a beautiful picture with a woman having butterfly wings! At that moment I knew that he was an Angel. Many times while praying, I have asked Jesus to make me like a butterfly, to be able to fly freely with butterfly wings to enjoy the outdoors... After receiving that particular picture he left.

Minutes later, Cathy and I went outside and look into both sides of the street but didn't see anyone. We asked Jesus if that man was an Angel, His response was a beautiful fragrance of fresh roses passing by our face. There were no Rose bushes around us or at a distance. His answer was clear.

Be not forgetful to entertain strangers: for thereby some have entertained angels unaware. Hebrews13:2 KJV

THE ANGEL AT THE PIZZA SHOP

On this occasion, I stopped to purchase a Pizza for a Family that I was visiting. Everything seemed normal nothing unusual. After sitting to wait for the Pizza, I noticed the man sitting next to me. He was waiting for his order.

I casually turn to Him and said hi, and noticed that he was wearing a cross around his neck. I comment about his beautiful cross and he thank me with a smile. At that moment I noticed his face features and hair. Something was different about him?

Suddenly I was aware of his uniqueness. He looked like a humble man. His hair didn't match any hairstyle that I have seen, difficult to put into words. Next thing, he excuses himself and walks outside the door. The only thing that he said was be right back.

I didn't pay attention to where he was going. Five minutes later he is back holding something wrapped on a white paper towel. He places the item on my hands saying, this is a Gift for you, and apologizes for the wrapping paper. I received the gift and begin to unwrap it. To my surprise I discovered a beautiful mirror with the Lord's Prayer written on the mirror, decorated in a very artistic way. The only thing that he said after I thanked him for the gift, was, "pray it daily" He got the Pizza and left.

Encounters with Angels in our daily lives...

THE BEGGAR WAS AN ANGEL

This happened during one of my Mission trips to Mexico.

Right after my arrival into Mexico, I was highly motivated to share the message that Jesus had given me for the trip. The Message was a Prayer for a brand new Life.
I was excited by watching how the people were thankful after receiving the prayer.

One week after my arrival, I realized that I was going to need more prayers? The following day, I got up early morning to converse with Jesus asking for his help and guidance.

That day, early afternoon, I asked one of my nephews, if he could take me to my Brother Alberto's house, and to stop at the bakery on our way. When we arrived at the Bakery, I got out of the car and ran inside quickly to save time.

On my way out of the bakery, I saw a beggar sitting at the steps wearing a big sombrero; I was unable to see his face. He extended his arm and opens his hand, at that moment I put some money on his hand, and he gave me a piece of paper with the other hand. I grab the paper and ran to the car.

After sitting inside the car, I opened the piece of paper, and discovered that it was a copy of a ten dollar bill and on the back was something written similar to the Prayers that I needed... Jesús said to me, make copies and give them out.

The following day, early morning, I was walking to the grocery store to get few things to fix breakfast for my brother and his daughter Tania. While walking to the store, I encountered an old friend of the family, and began to share what happened at the bakery the day before. When I was done sharing what happened, he said to me; "I have never seen a beggar outside the bakery, but I know where you can get the copies made. He said, my Son owns a Printing company, and is only three blocks away. He would gladly print them for you.

When I shared with my family about the beggar, their answer was the same, that they have never seen a beggar outside the bakery. After breakfast I took a walk to the printers and printed 700 copies.

After the copies were done, I asked Jesus to send me helpers to distribute the prayers. His answer was: walk to the corner of the street, where the Taxi drivers pick passengers, and stand there until some of them stop. And that's what I did. The taxis that stopped were my helpers. I would ask them if they could help me distribute the prayers and all of them said yes! I gave them a stack of prayers and left...

More helpers... it was morning time, when I was getting ready to go to the outside market to purchase fresh vegetables to make soup for lunch. When I opened the front door ready to leave, I heard a loud voice, selling something on the street. I waited to see what he was selling, and to my surprise, he had the kind of vegetables that I needed for the soup, and the vegetables were all cut up, ready to cook. I was being helped in many different ways!

I called the person selling the vegetables, and he stopped at the front door, and at that moment I ask him if I could give him a prayer? He quickly answered yes. I went inside to get the prayer and after getting the prayer, he said: if you need help distributing the prayers, I would gladly help you. At that moment I discovered that he was another helper send by Jesus!

By the time of my return to the United States, I had 70 prayers left. Praise God!!!

Jesus always arrives on time!

ANGELS DIALING MY PHONE CALLS

I remember wearing a long purple robe in the house to stay warm, and had the cordless phone inside my left pocket.

That day, I was conversing with Jesus, asking, to let me know when I should call my daughter. She was not feeling well.

This was the first time when the Angels began to dial my phone calls.

That morning, I was busy doing the daily chores in the house, when suddenly, I heard the sound of the phone dialing inside my pocket; after reaching the phone, I was surprised to discover that was dialing my daughter's phone number and it was ringing. At that moment I became aware that the Angels were making the phone call, because my cordless phone didn't even have her phone number recorded. The Angels knew her phone number for sure. My daughter didn't answer the phone, at that moment I ask Jesus for the reason for not answering the phone; He said that He wanted my daughter to know that I was thinking about her. This same Incident happened twice. My daughter answer the phone after the Angels dialed for the third time!

Five days later, the same incident happened, the phone was dialing inside my pocket,
And to my surprise, this time one of my Angels had dialed the phone number to a book store...Barnes and Nobles. So I ask Jesus to lead me to the books that He wanted me to buy. Sometimes I purchase books for me and other times are books to give to other people under his guidance. One of the book's titles is, Understanding the purpose and power of prayer. How to call Heaven into the Earth... and the other book title is: Understanding the purpose and power of women...

Life is fun and exciting when we can recognize when our Angels are helping in our daily lives.

ANGELS ARE WONDERFUL HELPERS...

I HEARD GOD'S VOICE SPEAKING

It happened while having a Near Death Experience, after giving birth to our son Peter.

That day, right after our Son was born, my body began to elevate. I was ascending without my physical body. I was watching my Spirit body detaching from the physical body. I had no fear, only a sense of Peace and Freedom.

Afterwards, I saw my spirit go into a Tunnel taking me into another Dimension. I watched my Spirit self traveling at high speed. After arriving into the other dimension I came out of the tunnel and entered a white cloud that was waiting for me. At that moment, I was embraced by the cloud and saturated with Love and Peace. Later on, I remember seeing my Father in that place, he was looking at me and smiling, but I couldn't get close to him... He had already died many years before.

The next thing that I saw was my spirit self, standing alone, and suddenly an arm with a white sleeve came out of nowhere, and a long narrow window appeared in front of me. At that moment the arm began to open the window. I remember stepping forward to get closer to the window, wanting to see the other side. What I saw was a glimpse of heaven, where everything is alive, a beautiful place difficult to describe with words.

After looking through the window, the same arm with the white sleeve came out and closed the window. Afterwards, I heard God's resounding voice asking, "Do you want to stay or go back" my Heavenly Father was giving me a choice. I wanted to stay, and at that instant, before giving my answer, I was reminded about our four children waiting for me at home, and decided to come back to care for my Family.

This experience prepared me for my mission on the Earth.

MARÍA DE JESÚS ALARCÓN L.

My experience with dreams while getting ready to travel for Mission work outside the country

On that occasion, I had collected many items from people that heard about my trip to Mexico. I took the items home and placed them in an empty room. After a while, I noticed that the pile was getting high... I have always traveled by plane, but this time I had many more things to take.

Couple days later, I ask Jesus about His plan for the trip. Jesus answered my request the following week. It was Saturday morning, 10-am, when the phone rang. At that moment I was asking Jesus for help, to discern the message given to me, by the dream that I had that night.

In the dream, I saw myself driving a Van with my good friend Antonio sitting beside me. Antonio was my helper. He took care of my property; I stood up and answered the phone, and recognized my friend Antonio's voice saying that he was selling his Van, asking if I would be interested to buying it. At that moment I was able to discern the dream that I had that night. Jesus was answering my prayer by providing transportation for the Trip.

After sharing with some of my friends about the many donations that I had received, they were concerned, and began to say that I was taking too many things. They said, that at the border "They are not going to believe that I am giving everything for free," and that I didn't even had any Credentials about working for God, and that I was not part of any Church in particular. That night, I conversed with Jesus thanking Him for providing everything that I needed for the trip.

Few days later, while checking the mailbox, I noticed a large white envelope; after opening the envelope, I discovered that I had received from Jesus a Certificate of Ordination as a Minister of God, and at that moment I thought, now I have proof that I work for God.

My last need was a driver. It was a long distance from Ohio to Mexico. And the way that Jesus provided for my need, is the following: It was a Wednesday afternoon. I was working late at the Municipal Court. I worked as a Spanish Interpreter and Probation Secretary. It was late afternoon, when a friend stopped to ask for advice in a legal matter. Afterwards, he asked if I was traveling to Mexico again, I said yes, but this time I am driving.

He asked, "Do you need someone to help you drive"? I said yes, He responded that he was planning to visit

Mexico and that his cousin was also available, and before leaving, we made plans to meet over the weekend to talk about it... during our visit we decided to travel together. Jesus had blessed me with two drivers... and we arrived into Mexico sooner than I expected.

I was blessed by having two drivers instead of one. God's ways are amazing!

The experience, when my eyes were directing my steps

That day, Jesus wanted me to go to a particular church that I didn't visit often. He said that he wanted me to give the prayer to the people that needed healing, and to do it, after the service. I asked him, how would I know the people that need healing? didn't hear an answer.

During the service, the Minister in the church suddenly stopped and asked the Congregation, that if anyone needed prayer for a healing, to stand up. After they stood up, I heard Jesus' voice saying, those are the ones. At the end of the service, I approach every single person and gave them the Prayer, and left.

I remember another occasion while stopping at the grocery store. That day, as soon as I parked the car, I began to perceive feelings of despair, disappointment and hopelessness. I was surprised by the feelings that appeared inside my heart almost instantly.

At that moment, I decided to ignore the feelings and entered the store focused on sharing the Prayer. that day, most of the people that I had asked if I could give them the prayer said yes, and thanked me for the prayer. Some of them would ask if they could give me a hug, saying that they needed the prayer at that moment, Only Jesus knew that.

After leaving the store, while walking towards my car, I became aware that six people hugged me after receiving the prayer, and noticed that the feelings I had earlier, before entering the store were gone.

A few days later, I was asking Jesus about the reason for the feelings that I had, before entering the grocery store. He said, the people that hugged me inside the store were experiencing those feelings, and after praying the Prayer, those feelings left. Jesus had arrived on time!

I love to be guided by Jesus daily, and watch how he reaches out to everyone in need every single day! Jesus always arrives on time in every situation.

I am thankful that I don't need to be perfect to earn his Love.

I would like to share another wonderful experience that happen in the Life of my friend

Antonio. God answered his simple prayer, and he received a supernatural ...answer.

He shared that one day, while attending a church service in Mexico; the Minister was speaking about the importance of helping in the church; by serving our Lord in gratitude for His love and provision. Antonio said, that later on before bed time, he was conversing with God regarding this issue, saying that he didn't have enough time to help in the church; that he needed to work to provide for his family.

Antonio approached father God, asking to increase his income and he would gladly help in the Church. Few days later, the answer arrived!

On that particular day, after getting home from work, he noticed that there was a small bird, a "yellow Canary," perched on the front porch of their house. He asked his wife Rosa about it. She answered, "The bird has been there all day." Antonio decided to place the bird inside a cage to protect him from getting hurt by other animals. The following day, two more Canaries arrived and once again they were placed inside the cage. Days later more birds, arrived.

Antonio said that they had to separate them to give them room to move. Not long after, they found two tiny eggs inside the cage. They moved them out and placed them in another new cage with a couple of adult birds. Days later, the two little eggs had hatched and new babies were born. In a short time they began to multiply, having more babies. Without saying a word about it, people began knocking at his door, to inquire about the birds, wanting to buy some of them.

Antonio said that for the price of one Canary, he was able to feed his Family of seven members for one day. Last time that I spoke to his wife Rosa, she said that the Canaries were still growing in size and quantity. This family lives in Mexico.

Jesus is faithful to answer our Prayers in unique ways, if it is for our good. No matter where we are, or where we live. Jesus is all over the world. And He can do the Impossible! His ways are exciting... The more we converse with Jesus, the Bigger he becomes inside our hearts...

All we need to do is to pray and reach out to Jesus for help sincerely, with our whole heart like children, believing that Jesus will give to us what we need. And remember that Jesus doesn't rush, but He's always on time!

And Jesus called a little child unto him, and set him in the midst of them, and said, verily I say unto you, except you be converted and become as little children, you shall not enter into the kingdom of heaven. Whosoever therefore shall humble himself as this little child, the same is greatest in the kingdom of heaven. Matthew 18: 2-3-4 KJV

When children ask God for what they want or need, they believe that Jesus (God) hears their prayer, they believe in His love for them, and patiently expect to receive what they want. It happened in our Family...

I clearly remembered the occasion when my granddaughter Lyndsey approached me, saying... Grandma, I want a baby sister, and I responded... ask our Lord Jesus. She was four years of age. Her parents didn't know that she wanted a baby sister.

During this time, Lyndsey had already prayed the Miracle Prayer with me. She had no doubt about having the little sister that she wanted, and we didn't talk about it, for a full year: until my daughter Rose announced her pregnancy, by saying that a baby sister was coming to join the family. I looked at Lyndsey and said, can you imagine how much Jesus loves you? He is giving you the little sister that you ask Him for. Her answer was: "Grandma, I prayed for her every night at bed time".

Now, her little sister Taylor is a beautiful young woman, and Lyndsey's best friend. Every time that I remind Taylor about how her sister wanted her to be part of the family, she smiles and runs towards Lyndsey, and gives her a Hug, thanking her for her prayers.

VISITING MEXICO WITH JESUS BY MY SIDE

I would like to share another experience, about God's ways of doing things.
It happened during mission work.

I remember that after my arrival in Mexico, family members where I was staying began to inquire about my Assignment for the mission trip. I shared that I didn't know what I was going to do, that Jesus had not revealed to me, His Plan for the trip. My answer was a surprise to them.

During my mission trips, the only thing that Jesus would let me know was about the place where I was going, the day of my departure, and what I needed to take with me.

Two days after my arrival, while waiting on Jesus for His instructions, my sister Alicia shared that while grocery shopping, she found an old friend of the family, her name was Bertha. (She is now in heaven) Bertha was one of God's precious Angels living on the Earth; fulfilling her personal Assignment… she was an amazing Gift to the world. Her Gift was similar to Mother Theresa of Calcutta; she was helping the Poor people.

While inside the grocery store, my sister Alicia made a comment about my visit in town to do mission work for Jesus, and before leaving the store, Bertha send me an invitation to a gathering for prayer on the following day, saying that she will be picking me up at my sister's house.

The following morning, after sharing with the family that Jesus wanted me to visit the Prisons, they instantly said No! That It was not a good thing. They said that the prisons in Mexico are very dangerous, and that most of the inmates are not inside a
Cell, they walk freely all over the place, and before entering the prison, the guards are in charge of checking every person, for guns, knives, drugs, etc., touching people's body all over. They could not believe that Jesus would want me to experience these kinds of things.

Was early afternoon, when Bertha arrived to my sister's house, to take me to the prayer group…While driving, Bertha began to ask about Jesus plans for my visit?

I said that early morning, while praying; Jesus told me, that his plan for me was to visit the Prisons, That He Wanted me to pray with the inmates for their salvation, and to let them know how much He loves them.

Now was my turn to ask about her Assignment. (Jesus has daily surprises if we stay close to him). After asking Bertha about her Assignment, her response was, "My Mission in the world given to me by my Creator is the Prisons" Wow, I was pleasantly surprised! I thought Lord Jesus, and you did it again, surprising me.

My friend Bertha said to me, I will be picking you up tomorrow early morning to visit the Prisons, and because we are entering together, they will not check you out at the entrance. **Jesus opens doors in unique ways...**

By now, we arrived at the location where we needed to be. It was very enjoyable being in a place where Jesus servants gather together to make plans to reach more people for His kingdom.

I traveled to Mexico a few more times before Bertha's departure to Heaven. While visiting the Prisons with Bertha, she would gather the inmates saying, Maria de Jesus

Has an important message for all of you from Jesus.

At times while visiting the prisons, I remember getting distracted by observing the surroundings inside the prison. On those occasions, I would ask in silence: "Lord Jesus what's the message?" Oh how glad I am, that in my Life, Jesus has always arrived on Time. Praise God!

The times that I spent in Bertha's presence, impacted my life, by observing her loving ways. She was a precious daughter of the living God with a huge kind Heart!

This wonderful woman adopted a pair of twin boys that were born inside the Prison. She said that the Prison was not a good place for children to grow up. And after their parents agreed for the children to be adopted, Bertha and her husband took the boys home, and care for them as their own.

On the exact day of Bertha's departure to Heaven, one of my clocks began to play the song Ave Maria. This particular clock hadn't played for many years until that particular day of her departure and after that day never played again.

THE PLAN FOR MY LIFE CONTINUED

Was the month of May, year-two thousand fifteen, when a new path for another mission appeared and began to unfold almost instantly? This particular assignment came by surprise revealing something unexpected.

That day seemed like an ordinary day until I opened the mailbox. While checking the mail I discovered a letter regarding animals and it took me by surprise while reading its content.

This was the beginning of Jesus' way to guide me into another part of my Assignment. After this particular day, I continued to receive mail from many different states regarding the same issue, the animals.

This became a regular routine. I would get the letters, read them and place them inside a large bag. Most of the letters had pictures with abused animals.

My heart was impacted by reading and seeing what was happening to the animals. There were times when I was unable to sleep after looking at some of the pictures. I consider the animals to be part of our Heavenly family.

Did you know that God created the animals before he created us, the human race?

During this time, while speaking with family members and friends, I would ask if they were getting this kind of mail. And all of them replied, "No, I am not." And at this point, I began to search for answers.

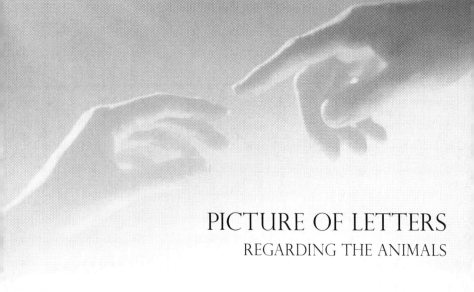

PICTURE OF LETTERS
REGARDING THE ANIMALS

And now, I knew that Jesus was speaking directly to me about something that was important to Him. I began to consult the Bible (King James Version) to discern the message. He guided me to the book of Genesis, and I begin to read about the beginning of God's Creation.

God said, Let the Earth bring forth the living creatures after his kind, cattle and creeping thing, and beast of the earth after his kind; and it was so. And God made the beast of the earth after his kind, and cattle after their kind, and everything that creepeth upon the earth after his kind; and God saw that it was good.
Genesis 1:24-25 KJV

After reading the first chapter of Genesis, the first thing that I became aware, was the fact that God created all of the animals before humans. Right then I could see that the animals are very important to God. The Noah's Ark also reveals God's love for the animals. God gave specific instructions to Noah regarding the animals; he wanted to make sure that there were pairs of every kind inside the Ark. He wanted the animals to reproduce.

Now, I was able to clearly see the love that God has for the Animals, God's Love has no measure. Our Creator is not only a Loving God; He is the Essence of Love!

And God said; Let us make man in our image, after our likeness: and let them have dominion over the fish of the sea, and over the fowl of the air and over the cattle, and over all the earth, and over every creeping thing that creepeth upon the earth. Genesis 1:26 KJV

So God created man in his own image, in the image of God created him; male and female created them. Genesis 1:27 KJV

And God blessed them, and God said unto them, be fruitful, and multiply, and replenish the earth, and subdue it: and have dominion over the fish of the sea, and over the fowl of the air, and over every living thing that moves upon the earth. Genesis 1:28 KJV and God said, Behold, I have given you every herb bearing seed, which is upon the face of all the earth, and every tree, in which is the fruit of the tree yielding seed; to you it shall be for meat! Genesis 1:29 KJV

And to every beast of the earth, and to every fowl of the air, and to every thing that creepeth upon the earth, wherein there is life, I have given every green herb for meat and it was so! And God saw every thing that he had made, and behold, it was very good. And the evening and the morning were the sixth day. Genesis 1:30-31 KJV...

A revelation is coming to me; saying that since the beginning of time, the animals were not created to be for food. The killing of animals to have as a meal began when Sin entered the world by Adam and Eve's disobedience.

And after our Salvation, when we become born again Christians, we receive a brand new life without the original Sin, and now we follow God's instructions given to us since the beginning of time.

And God said, Behold, I have given you every herb bearing seed, which is upon the face of all the earth, and every tree, in which is the fruit of the tree yielding seed; to you it shall be for meat. Genesis 1:29 KJV

Jesus words: Verily I say unto you, this generation shall not pass away, till all is fulfilled. Heaven and earth shall pass away: but my words shall not pass away.
Luke 21:32-33 KJV

By Jesus dying on the Cross-for our Sins, means that our lives have been saved and redeem…and we have received a brand new life. All of our Sins from the past life, have been forgiven and removed from us, and now, we have become born again by Jesus Crucifixion and Resurrection.

Jesus answered and said unto him, verily, verily, I say unto thee, except a man be born again, he cannot see the kingdom of God. John 3: 3-7 KJV

Now, I was aware that from the beginning of time, God did not plan for us to eat animal meat. Our bodies were not created to consume that kind of meat.

God's Creation… People and Animals, living on the Earth are not equipped to eat meat. Our body was not made to process animal meat since the beginning of time.

Since the beginning of our Creation, God made us aware about what we should eat, He knows what is best for us, and He is our maker.

Have you noticed that when we do fasting, avoiding eating meat, our connection with the Holy Spirit is much stronger?

In my own Family, I have experienced some losses. One of them was a brother who loved eating meat. At one point in his life, he became very ill. His Doctor recommended that he stop eating meat because his body had accumulated too much uric acid. My brother stopped eating meat for one year. After a year, he was saying to family members, that he was feeling like new again, and after a short time later; temptation arrived in his life through his tongue. His taste buds reminded him about the taste of meat. My brother started to eat meat once again and after a short time he died instantly. He was a young man.

My heart is deeply touched by being aware about Our Heavenly Father, taking time to inform all of us about this important Issue. His desire for us is to be in good health to live an abundant Life. I am amazed about God's love for all of us.

The thief cometh not, but to steal, and to kill, and to destroy: I have come that they might have life, and that they might have it more abundantly. I am the good shepherd: the good shepherd gives his life for the sheep. Jesus said: I have come that they might have life, and have it more abundantly John 10:10-11 KJV

The letters regarding the animals continued to come into my mail box, and this time to my surprise, was about a different issue. They were asking for donations to help with the training of dogs that helped handicap people.

Now, I became aware that everyone and everything on the Earth has a personal Mission to fulfill. People, Animals, Trees, the Sun, the Moon, the Appliances in our homes, our Shoes, our Cars, etc., every good thing, has been made with a purpose by a Wise Creator.

I remember one day when I needed to do some ironing. I plugged the iron cord and waited for the iron to reach the right temperature. I left the room for few minutes. When I got back, the iron was cold. I noticed a phone number on the iron, saying to call in case of any kind of need. I called the number and explained my problem, the man who answered ask "give me the Iron's number, after a few minutes he came back to the phone and said, when this particular iron stops getting warm, it cannot be repaired.

The revelation was that the Iron worked throughout its life, fulfilling the given mission until the end.

This also happens with us. All of us have arrived from Heaven holding a Gift to share with the world. The Gift is our personal Mission to discover and to fulfill until is time for us to go to our Heavenly home.

If we use the animals for food none of us will benefit by it. Our health will suffer by eating something that was not meant for us to eat. The Animals will suffer by dying before their time and both of us will be unable to fulfill our Assignments. Everything that God has created is important to Him. All of us have an important mission to fulfill here on the Earth. Our Heavenly Father knows what He is doing all of the time.

I would like to share that the beginning of my awareness regarding this issue… began about thirty three years ago when my daughter Anne spoke to me about it. She read the word of God to me, beginning in Genesis… and at that moment, I was convinced that it was a revelation from Jesus, and part of my assignment.

Since then, I began to eat according to God's word. My daughter Anne started to follow God's word since the age of ten, and now she has graduated in Nutrition…

DANIEL AND HIS FRIENDS OBEYED GOD

The word of God says in the book of Daniel, that Daniel and his friends… three young men, were elected to be trained and tested to be able to serve in the Kings palace,.

And the king appointed them a daily provision of the king's meat, and of the wine which he drank; and nourishing them for three years. Daniel 1: 5 KJV.

But Daniel purposed in his heart that he would not defile himself with the portion of the king's meat, or with the wine which he drank. 1: 8 KJV

Daniel asked to be tested for ten days, with only vegetables to eat and water to drink. Daniel 1:12 KJV.

And at the end of ten days, their countenances appeared better and fatter in flesh than all the young men who ate the portion of the king's meat.
Daniel 1:15 KJV.

After the ten days, they were allowed to be nourished with vegetables and water. Daniel 1:16 KJV

I recommend reading the Book of Daniel for more information, beginning with Chapter One, until you discover all about Daniels life. His Assignment was very amazing.

I encourage you to pray for discernment regarding this issue.

It was early morning, still in bed, when Jesus began to answer the question that I had on my mind... the question was about the reason why some of us are not interested to hear or think about the suffering of animals being killed for the benefit of some of us, wanting to eat meat.

The way that I understood his answer was: not having enough love in our hearts for us and others. I remember when I discovered that I didn't love myself. It happens while participating in a spiritual retreat. One of the leaders at the retreat asks me a question that was difficult to answer. He asked who Maria is? At that moment tears began to flow down my face, my whole life I have been a daughter a mother, a spouse a sister, a friend. But I didn't know who I was? I was asked what do you like to eat, my answer was, what my children and husband like to eat. Is there anything that you enjoy doing? I was unable to answer... I had no idea of anything that I enjoy doing... I discover that I forgot to love myself, and all I did was crying. I gave my love and time away to others and didn't have enough love and time left for myself.

During my first Retreat, Jesus was preparing me to receive a brand new life, by healing my wounds and erasing painful memories... He was giving me a new start. It was the Beginning of loving me, and loving my Lord and Savior...

Authentic Love is an expression revealing the presence of God living within us, inside our hearts...

When we find Jesus, and His Salvation, we can recognize the love that God has for us, personally and for all of his Creation. We suddenly begin to see everything that God created with different eyesight... we discover inside our hearts the tender love that our Creator has for all of us!

The warmed of his Love and the Peace that we receive within us, motivates us to be the best that we can be, filled with desire to please Him, by helping others in need.

In one occasion, I was inspired to write the following words after speaking and praying with homeless people walking on the streets...

CRYING HEARTS
SEARCHING FOR JESUS

Every time I see a homeless person walking on the streets, looking around as if searching for something feeling incomplete... I wonder?

I wonder if they are searching for a smile, a hug or for someone who would listen, to
A story of a broken heart... I wonder?

I wonder if they were hugged by their parents, their grandma and grandpa.

I wonder what their hearts are trying to share. I wonder if their tears reveal regret.
I wonder?

Or perhaps, their need is about hearing words that would motivate, to search for the missing link, the reason for living on the Earth.

I wonder, how many of us remember Jesus words:

When he saw the crowds, He was moved with compassion for them, because they were harassed and helpless, like sheep without a shepherd.

Then He said to his disciples, "The harvest truly is plentiful, but the Laborers are few.
Therefore pray to the Lord of the harvest to send out laborers into His harvest."

Matthew 9:37-38

Jesus words: I Jesus has sent MY angel to testify to you these things in the churches. I am the Root and the Offspring of David, the bright and Morning Star. Revelation 22:16 KJV

Printed in the United States
By Bookmasters